W9-BWX-459

Patriotic Gems

ISBN 0-7935-2178-5

HAL•LEONARD® CORPORATION

7777 W. BLUEMOUND RD. P.O. BOX 13819 MILWAUKEE, WI 53213

Patriotic Gems

CONTENTS

AMERICA
(My Country, 'Tis Of Thee)

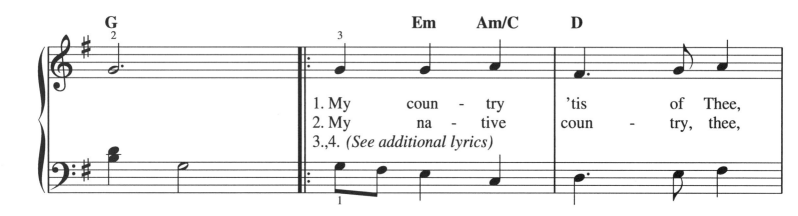

1. My coun - try 'tis of Thee,
2. My na - tive coun - try, thee,
3.,4. *(See additional lyrics)*

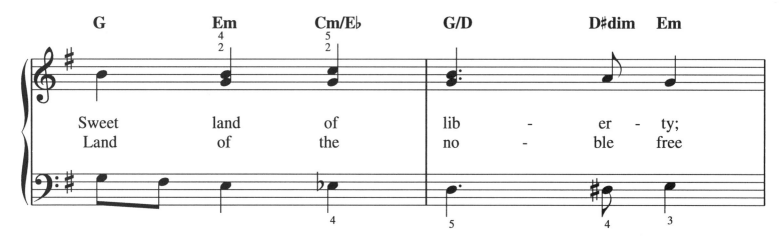

Sweet land of lib - er - ty;
Land of of the no - ble free

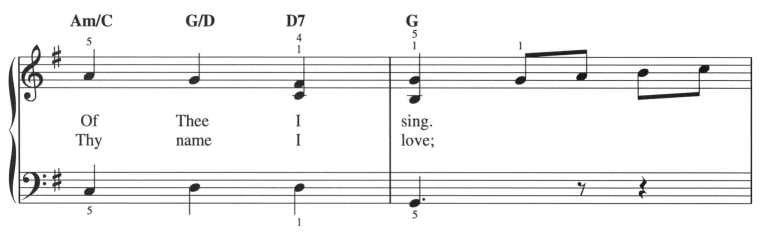

Of Thee I sing.
Thy name I love;

5

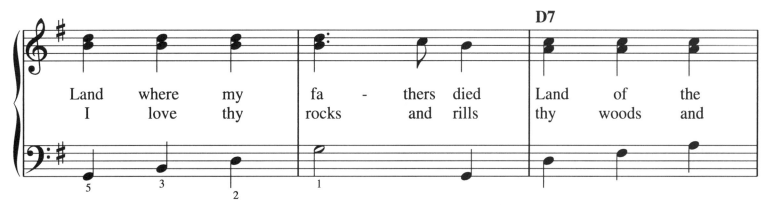

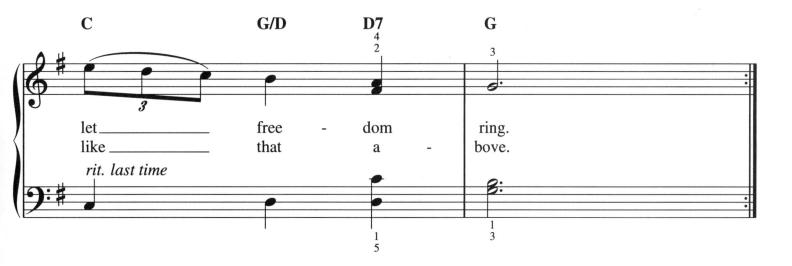

Additional Lyrics

3. Let music swell the breeze
   And ring from all the trees
   Sweet freedom's song.
   Let all that breathe partake
   Let mortal tongues awake
   Let rocks their silence break
   The sound prolong.

4. Our fathers' God, to thee
   Author of liberty
   To Thee we sing
   Long may our land be bright
   With freedom's holy light
   Protect us by thy might,
   Great God, our King

AMERICA, THE BEAUTIFUL

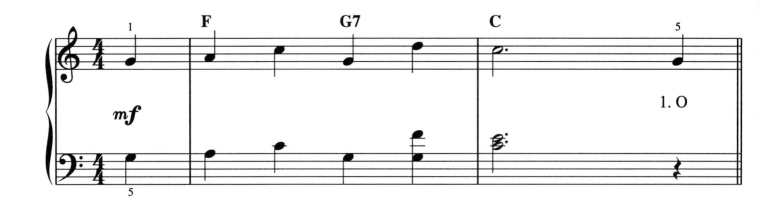

1. O

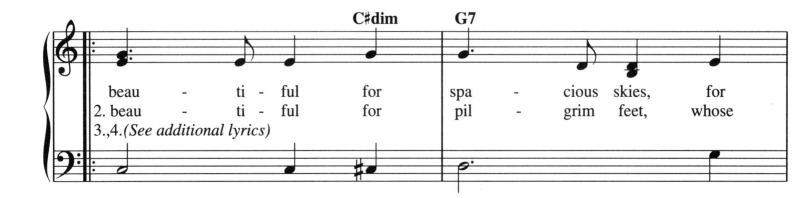

beau - ti - ful for spa - cious skies, for
2. beau - ti - ful for pil - grim feet, whose
3.,4.*(See additional lyrics)*

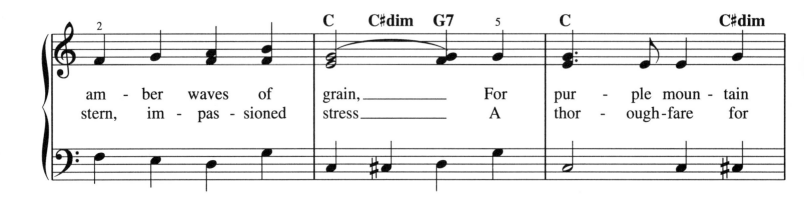

am - ber waves of grain,_____ For pur - ple moun - tain
stern, im - pas - sioned stress_____ A thor - ough-fare for

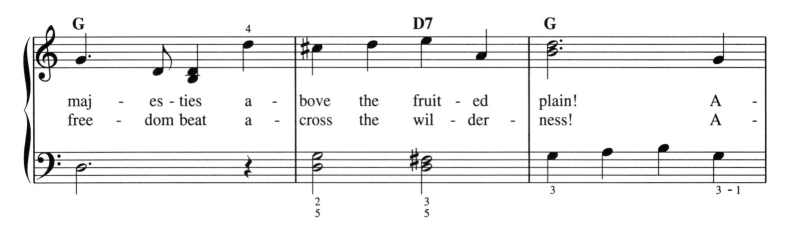

maj - es - ties a - bove the fruit - ed plain! A -
free - dom beat a - cross the wil - der - ness! A -

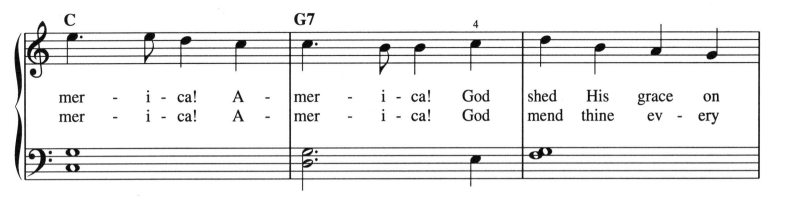

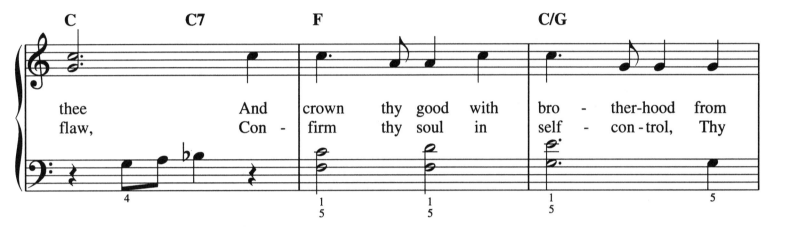

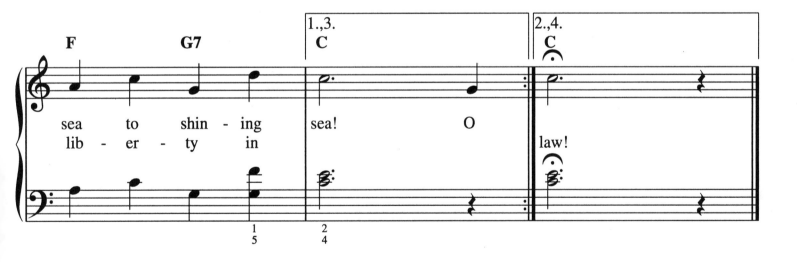

Additional Lyrics

3. O beautiful for heroes proved in liberating strife,
   Who more than self their country loved, and mercy more than life!
   America! America! May God thy gold refine,
   Till all success be nobleness and every gain divine!

4. O beautiful for patriot dream that sees beyond the years
   Thine alabaster cities gleam undimmed by human tears!
   America! America! God shed His grace on thee,
   And crown thy good with brotherhood from sea to shining sea!

AMERICAN PATROL

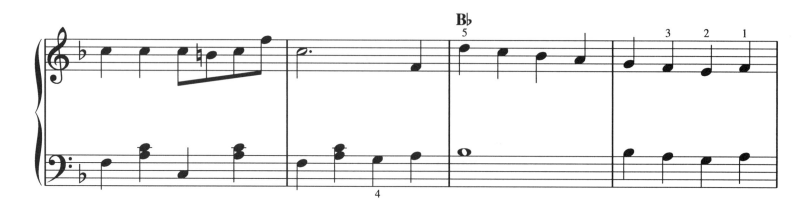

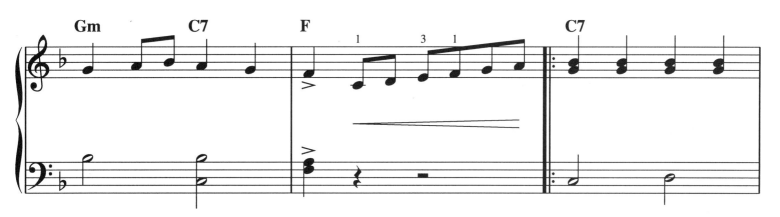

ANCHORS AWEIGH

Bright march tempo

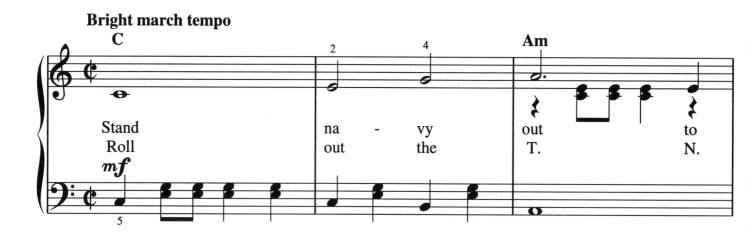

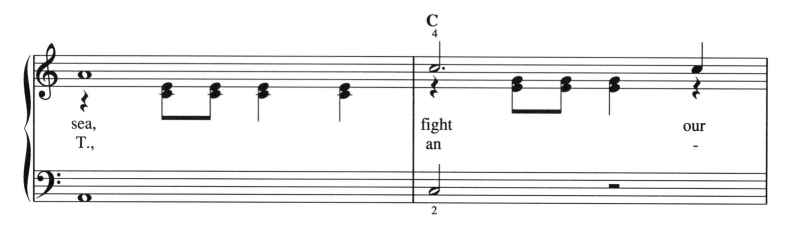

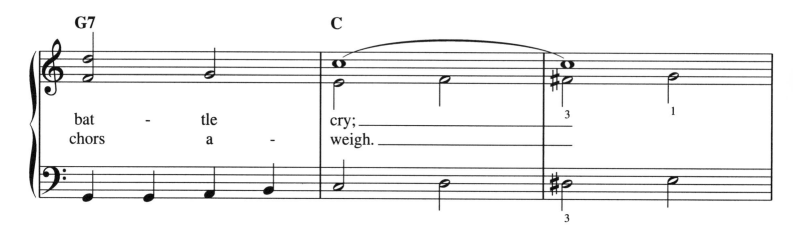

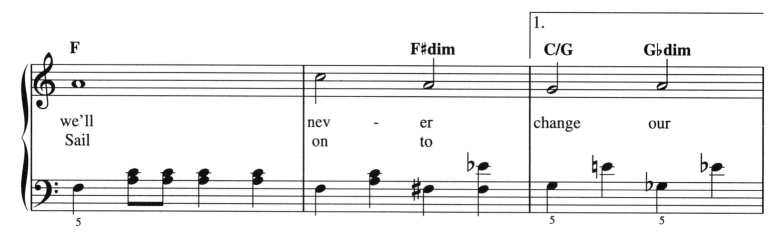

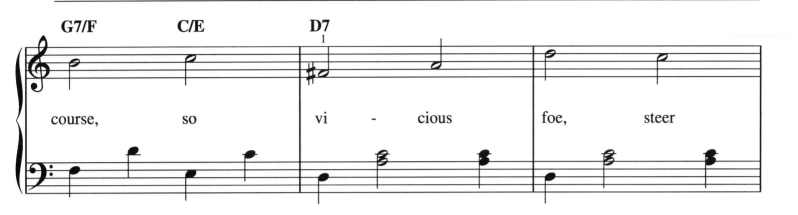

course, so vi - cious foe, steer

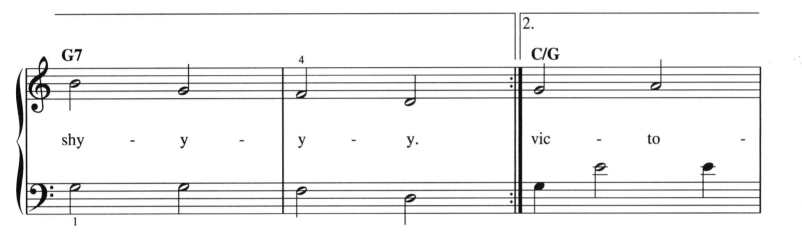

shy - y - y - y. vic - to -

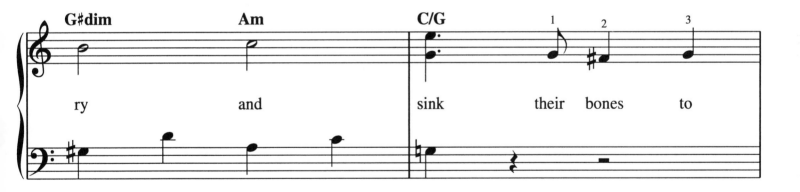

ry and sink their bones to

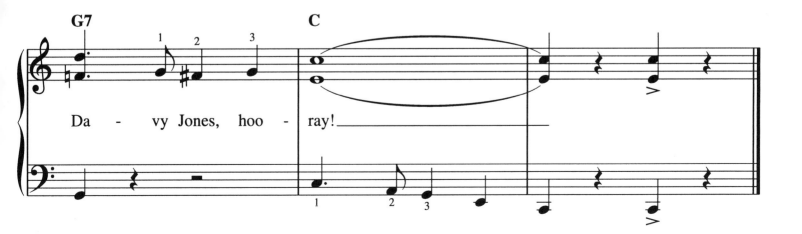

Da - vy Jones, hoo - ray! ____

THE BATTLE CRY OF FREEDOM

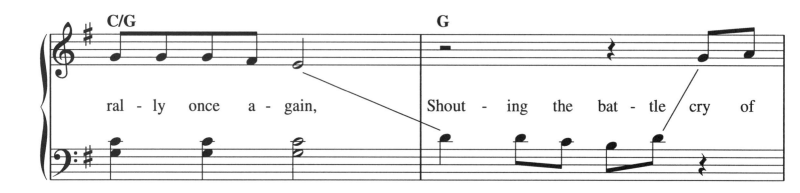

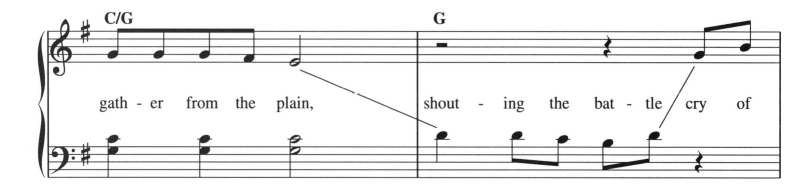

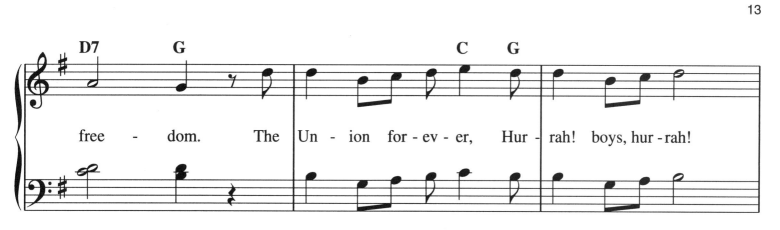

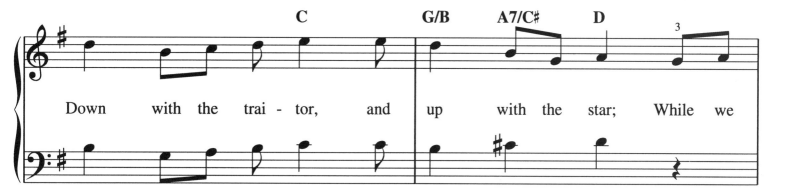

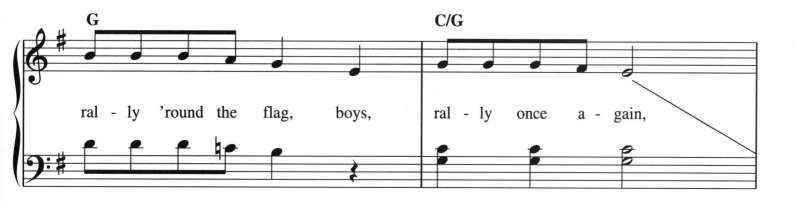

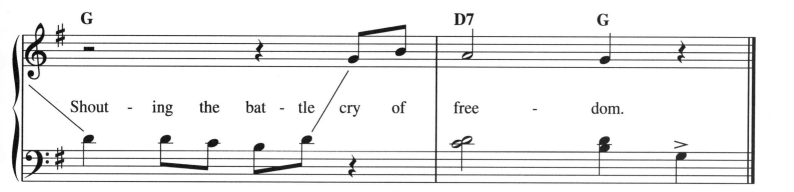

BATTLE HYMN OF THE REPUBLIC

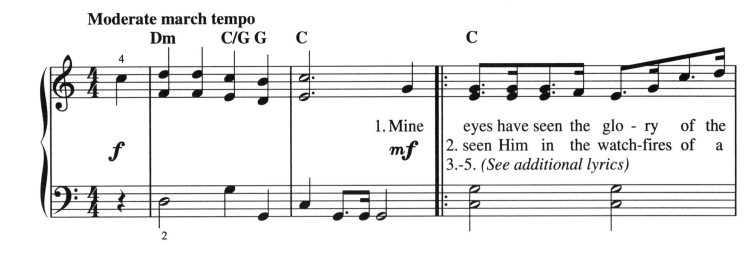

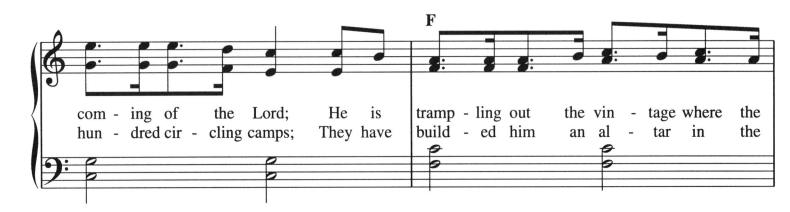

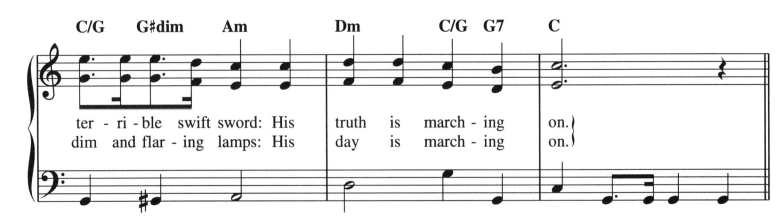

Additional Lyrics

3. I have read a fiery gospel writ in burnished rows of steel:
   "As ye deal with my condemners, so with you my grace shall deal;
   Let the Hero, born of woman, crush the serpent with his heel,
   Since God is marching on."
   To Chorus:

4. He has sounded forth the trumpet that shall never call retreat;
   He is sifting out the hearts of men before His judgement seat:
   Oh, be swift, my soul, to answer Him! be jubilant, my feet!
   Our God is marching on.
   To Chorus:

5. In the beauty of the lilies, Christ was born across the sea,
   With a glory in His bosom that transfigures you and me:
   As He died to make men holy, let us die to make men free,
   While God is marching on.
   To Chorus:

THE CAISSONS GO ROLLING ALONG

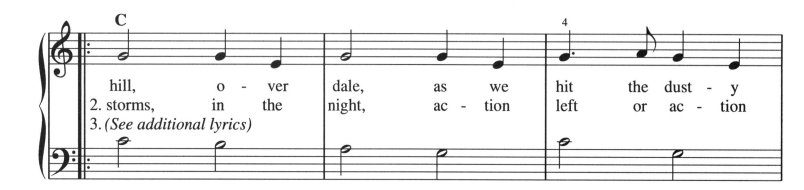

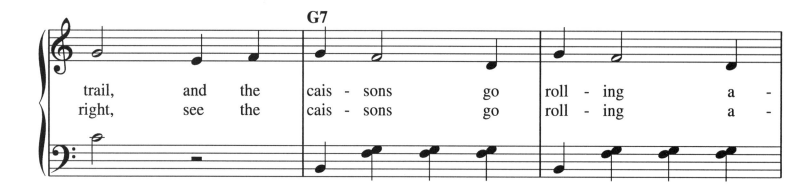

shout coun - ter | march and right a - | bout, And the
rear. Pre - pare to | mount your can - non - | eer, and the

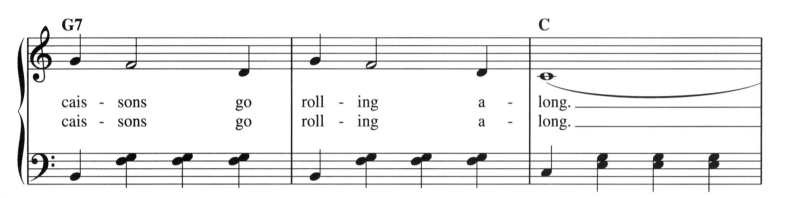

G7   **C**

cais - sons go | roll - ing a - | long. _____
cais - sons go | roll - ing a - | long. _____

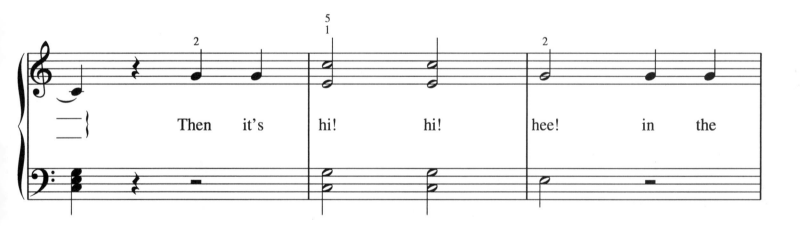

Then it's | hi! hi! | hee! in the

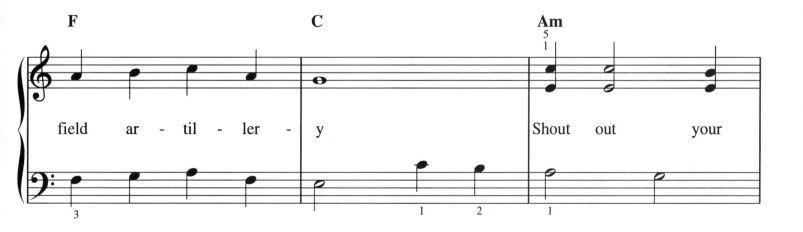

F   **C**   **Am**

field ar - til - ler - y | | Shout out your

18

num - bers loud and strong. *(One two!)* For where - e'er you

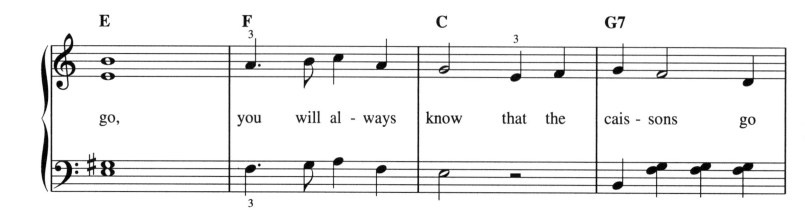

go, you will al - ways know that the cais - sons go

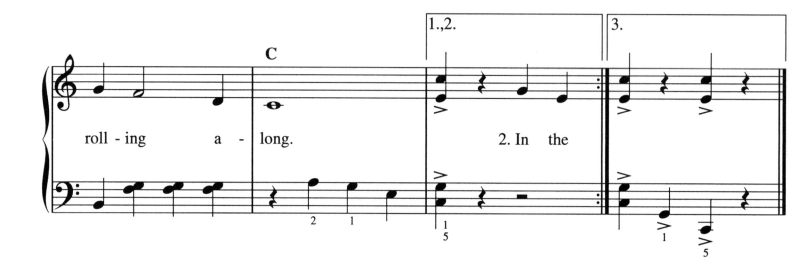

roll - ing a - long. 2. In the

Additional Lyrics

3. On the front, day and night, where the doughboys dig and fight,
And the caissons go rolling along.
Our barrage will be there, fired on the rocket's flare,
As those caissons go rolling along.

COLUMBIA, THE GEM OF THE OCEAN

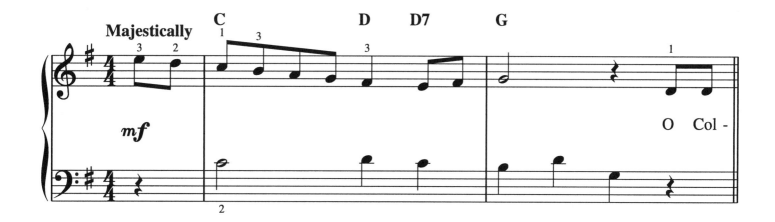

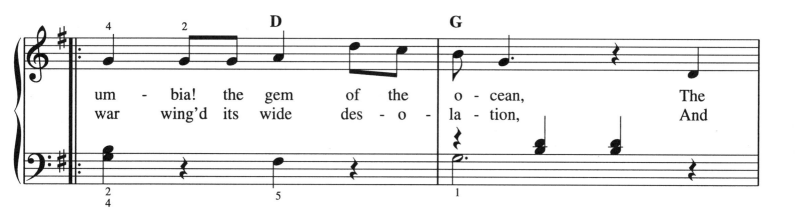

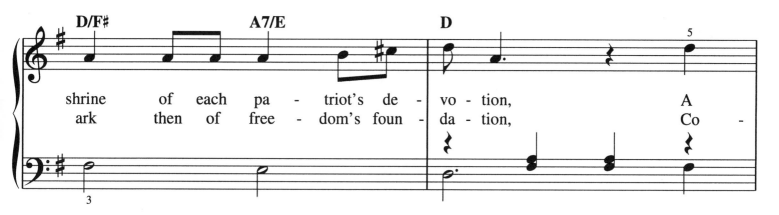

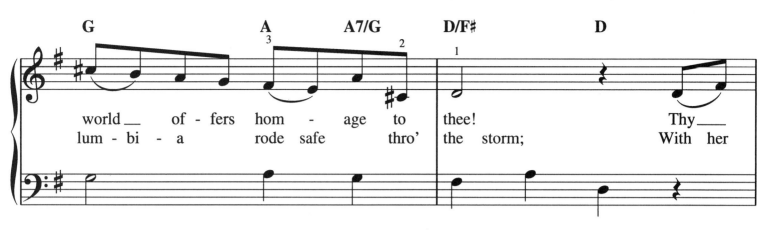

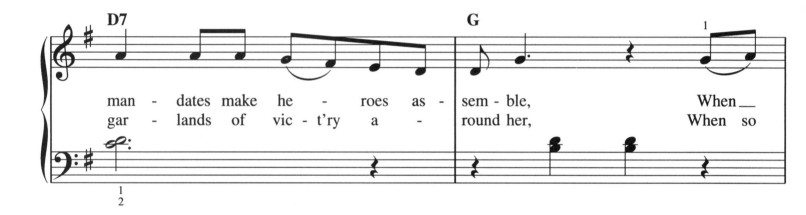

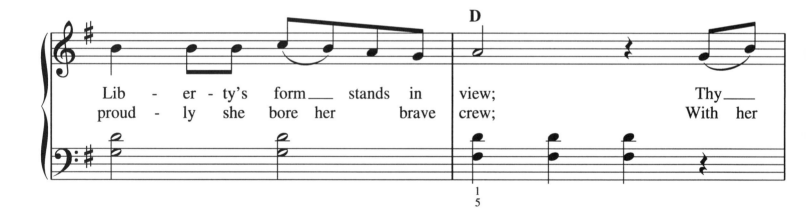

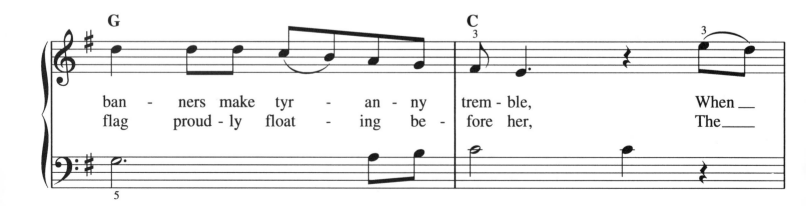

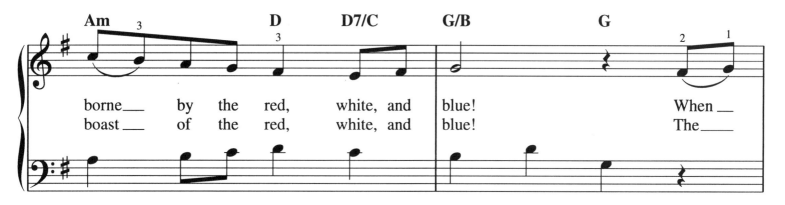

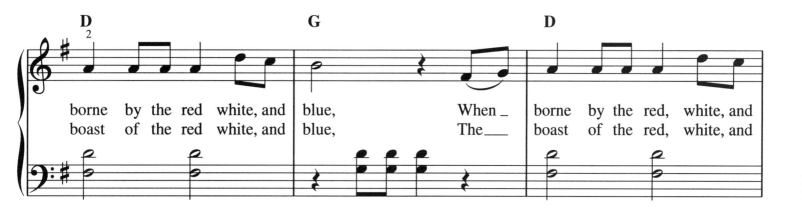

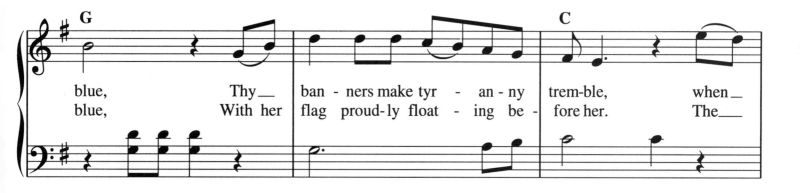

HAIL TO THE CHIEF

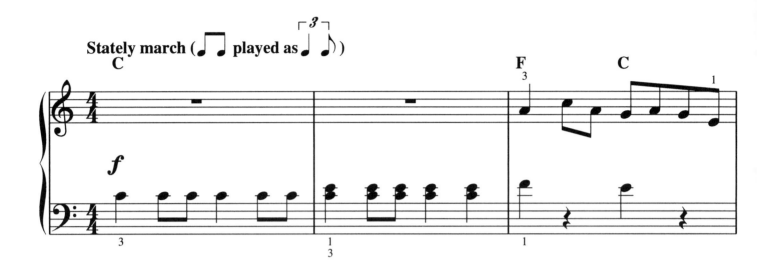

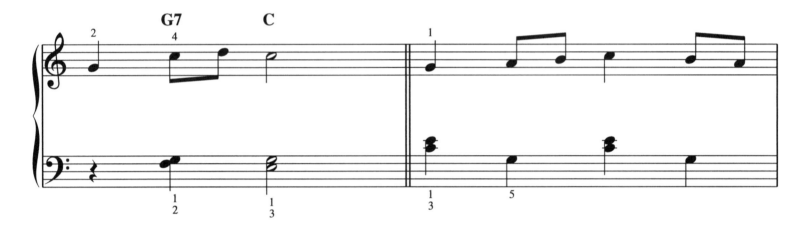

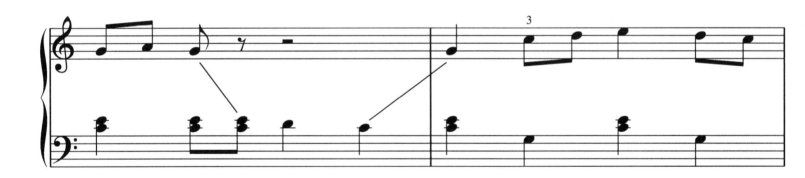

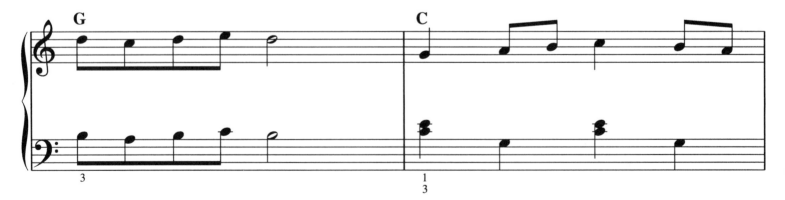

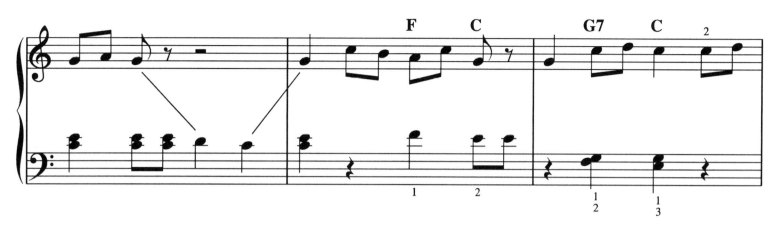

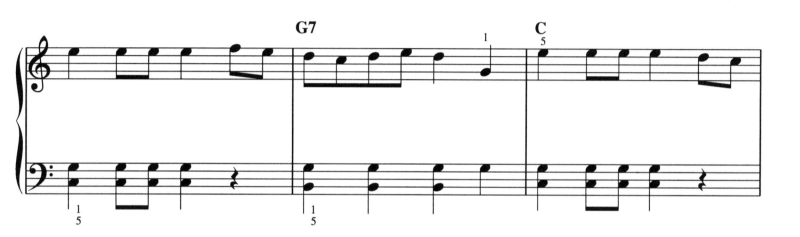

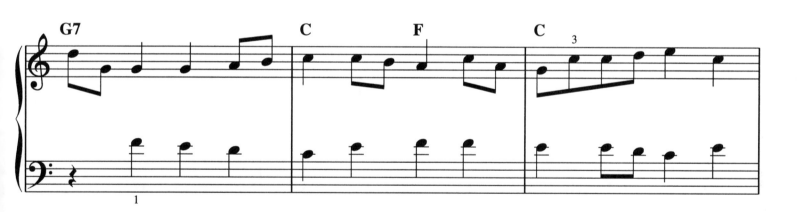

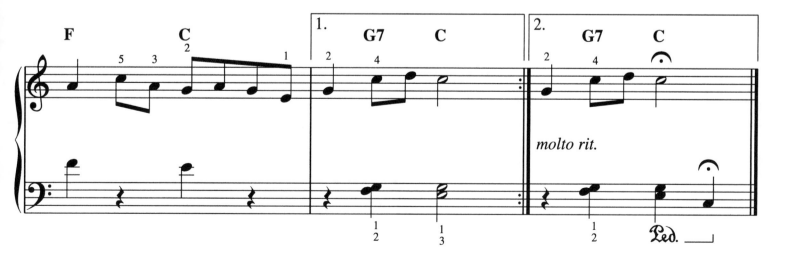

THE LIBERTY BELL

Moderate march tempo

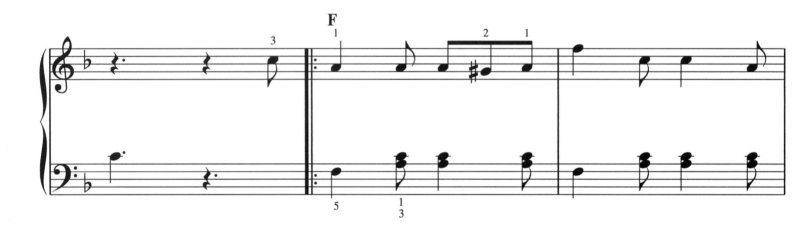

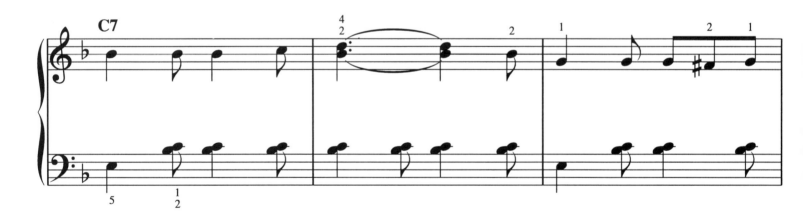

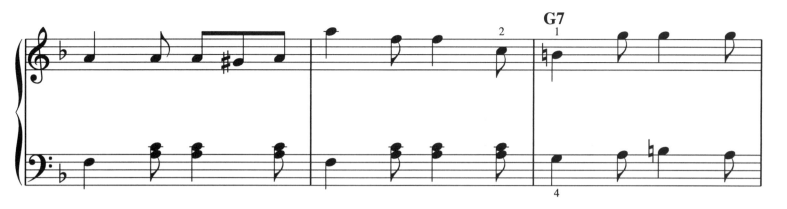

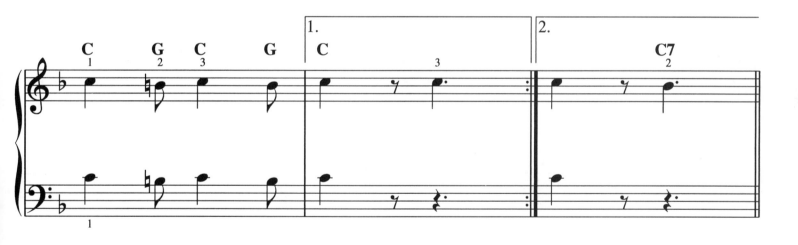

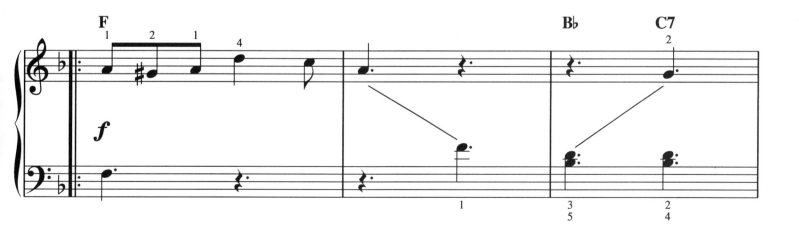

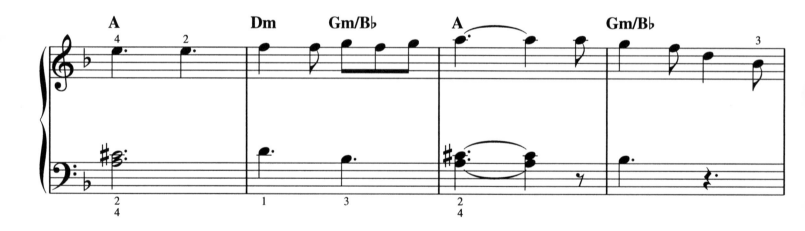

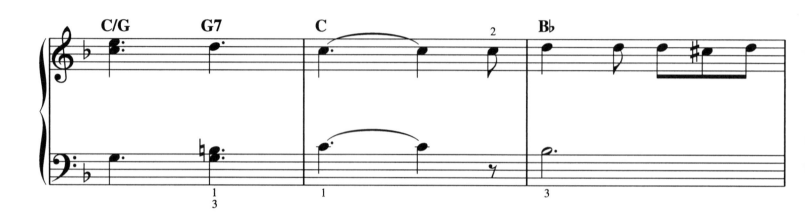

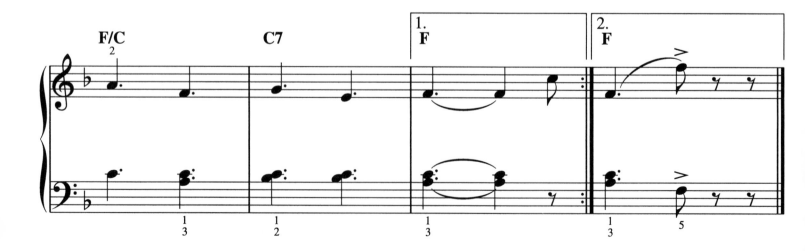

SEMPER FIDELIS

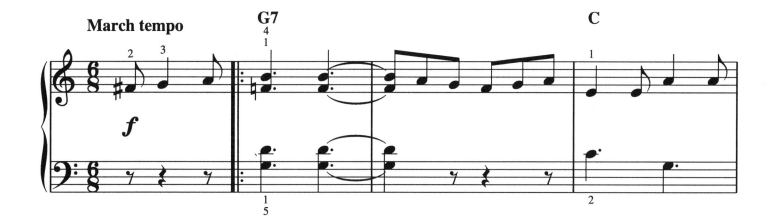

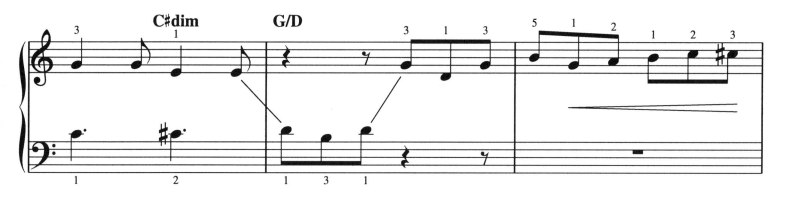

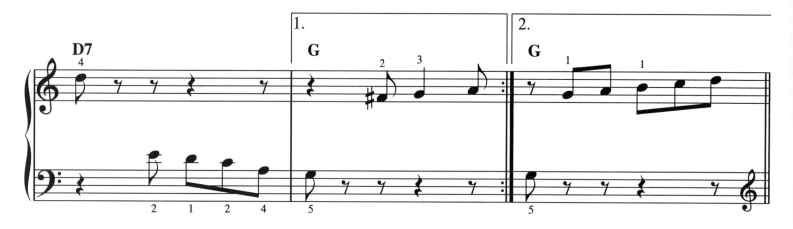

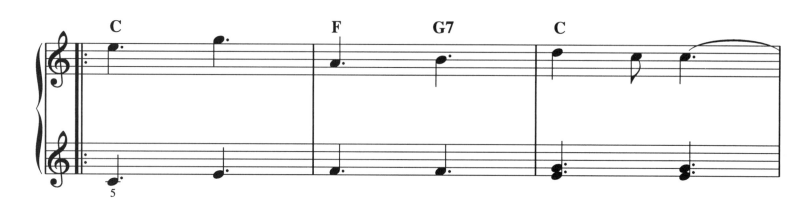

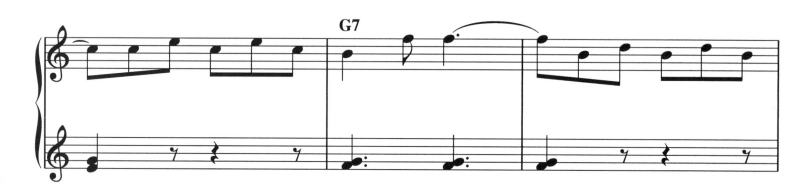

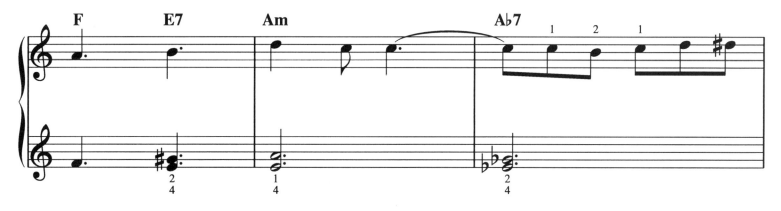

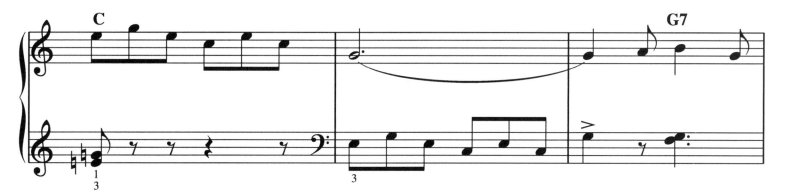

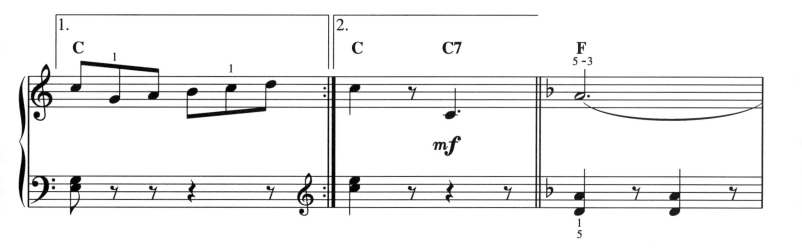

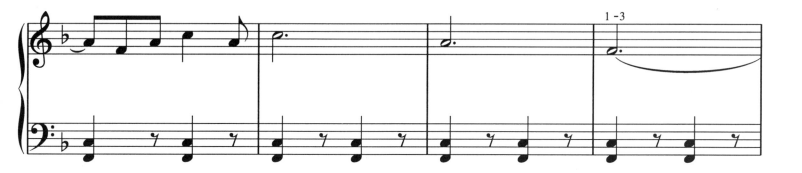

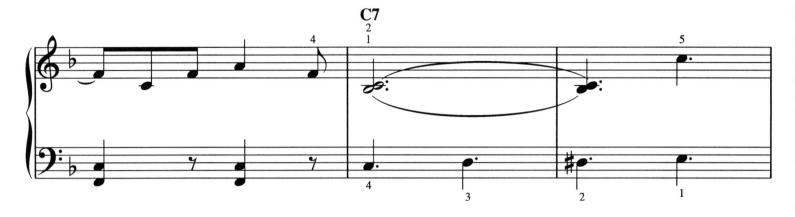

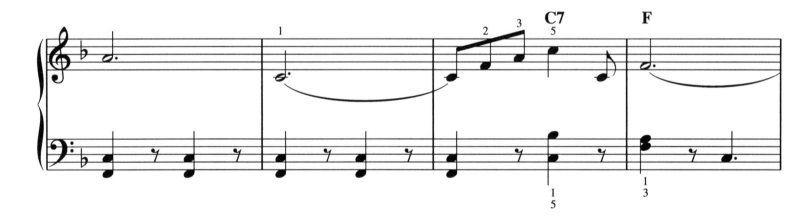

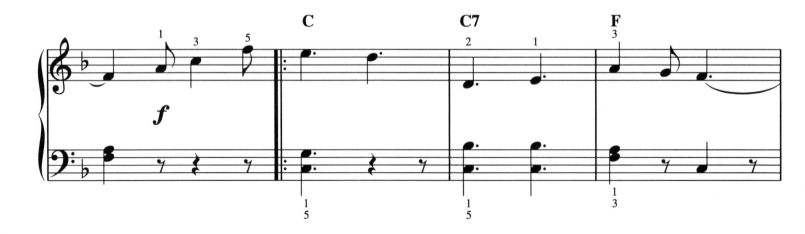

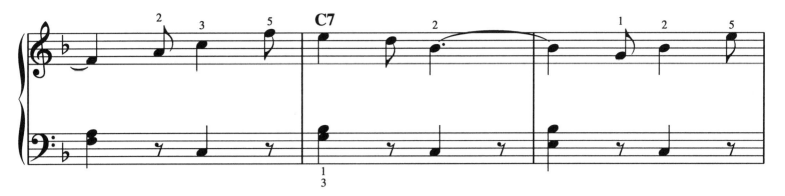

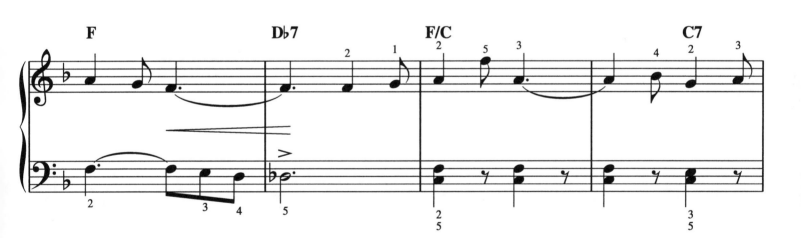

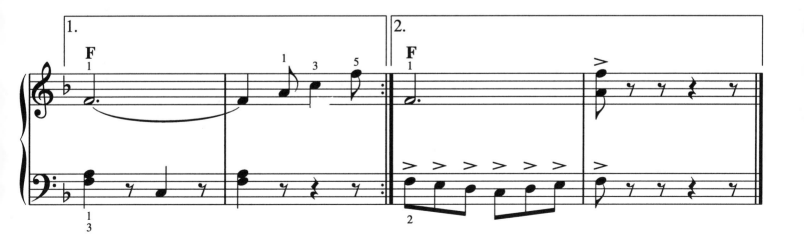

THE MARINE'S HYMN

Steady march tempo

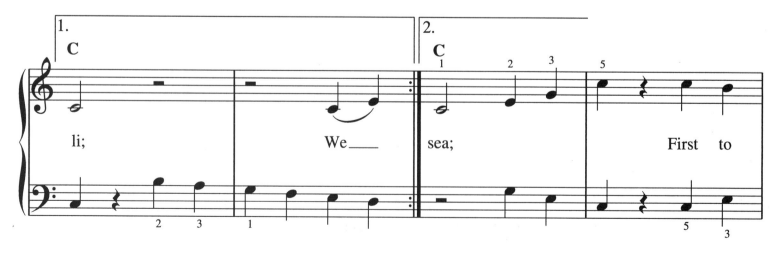

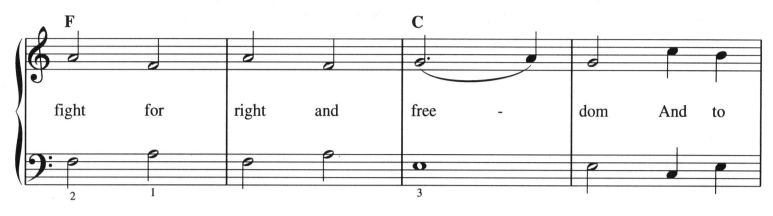

fight for right and free - dom And to

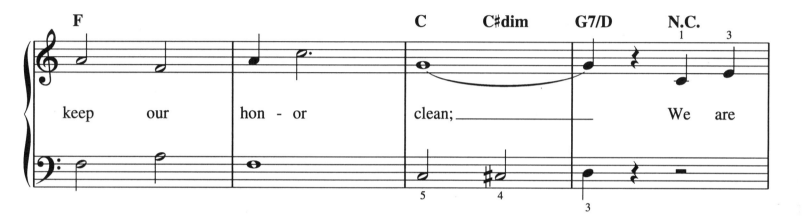

keep our hon - or clean; We are

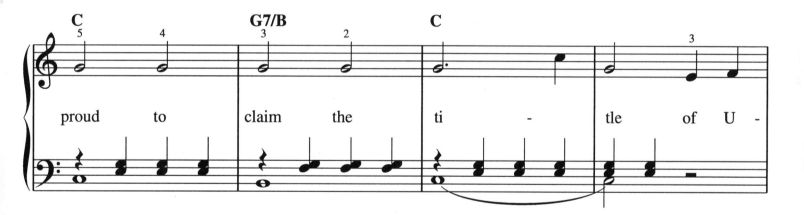

proud to claim the ti - tle of U -

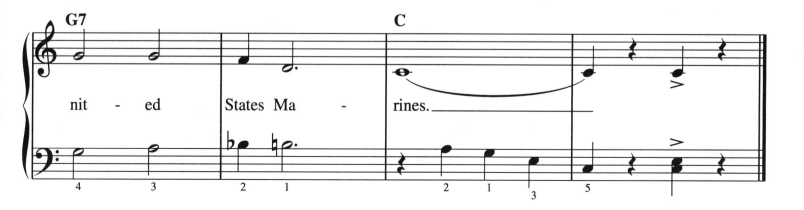

nit - ed States Ma - rines.

ONWARD, CHRISTIAN SOLDIERS

Like a slow march

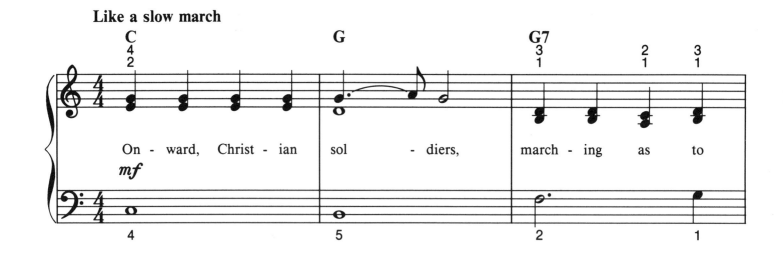

On - ward, Christ - ian sol - diers, march - ing as to

mf

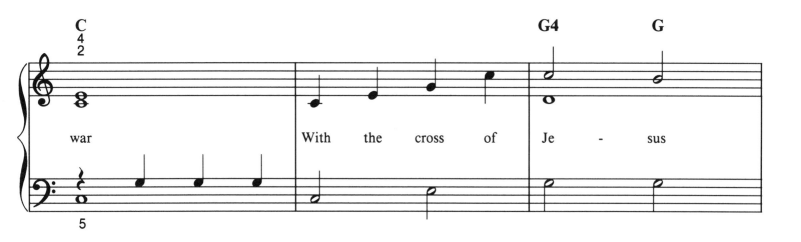

war   With the cross of Je - sus

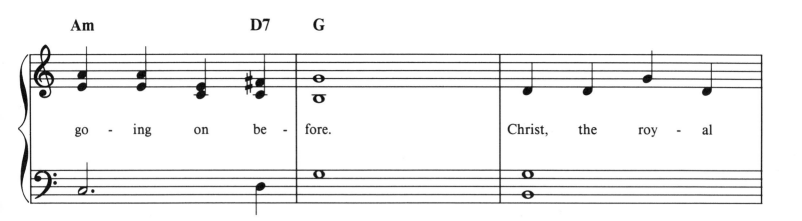

go - ing on be - fore.   Christ, the roy - al

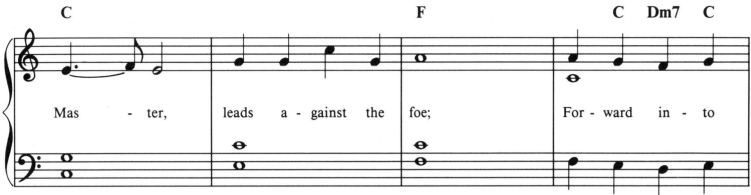

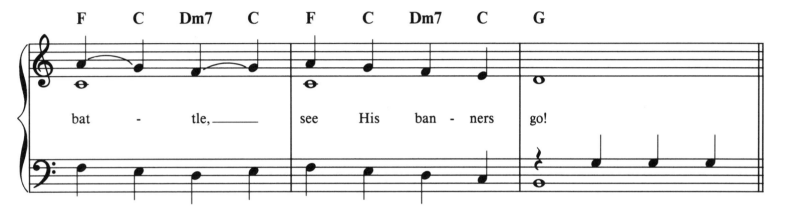

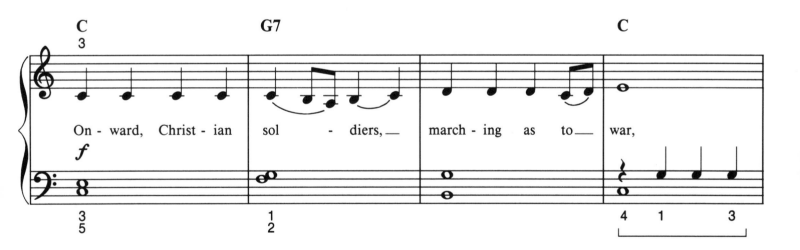

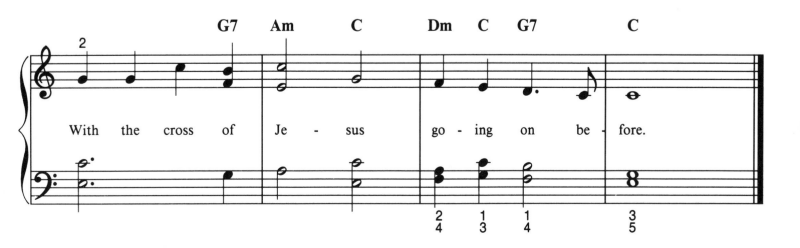

OVER THERE

Moderate march

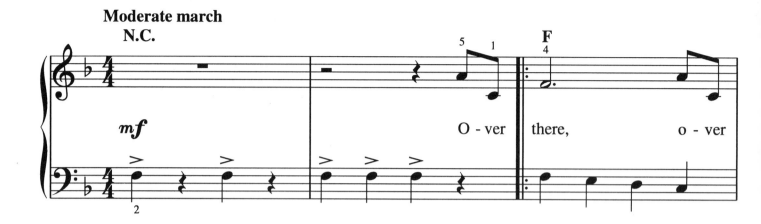

O - ver there, o - ver

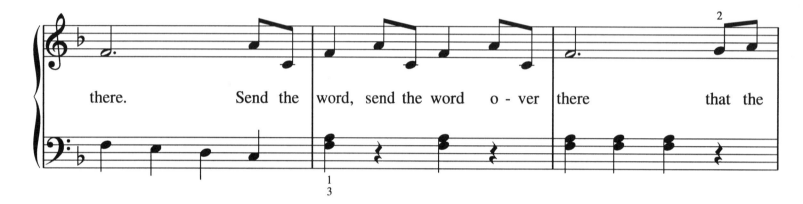

there. Send the word, send the word o - ver there that the

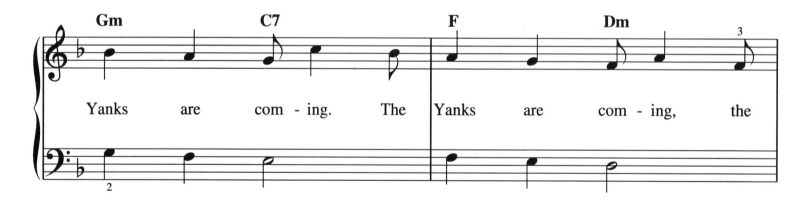

Yanks are com - ing. The Yanks are com - ing, the

drums rum - tum - ming ev - 'ry - where. So pre -

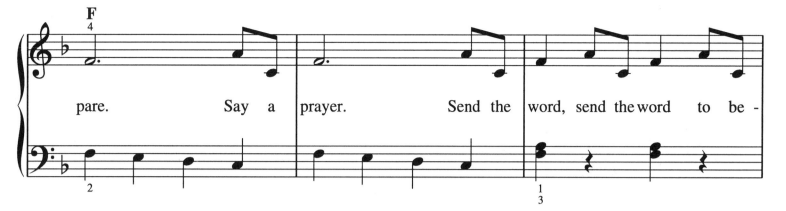

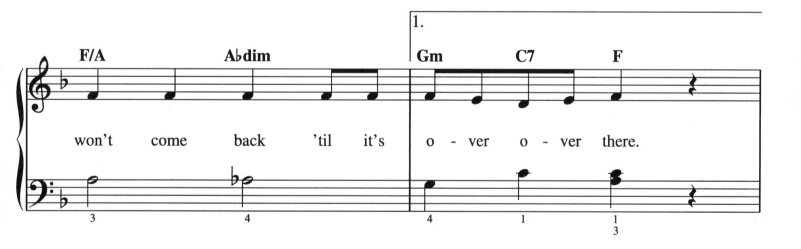

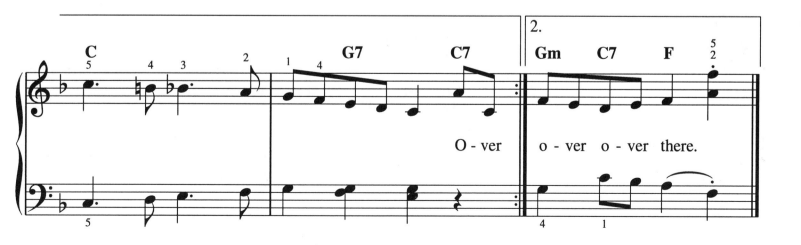

THE STAR-SPANGLED BANNER

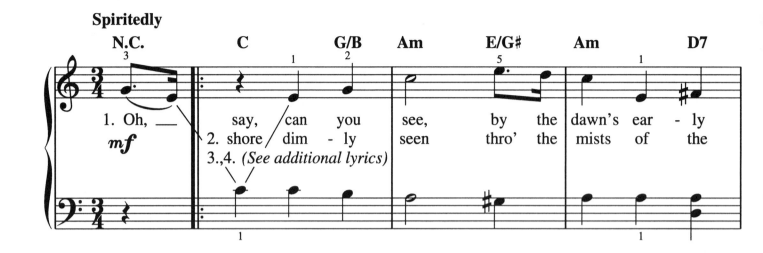

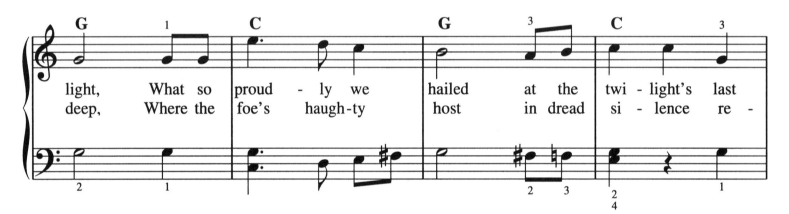

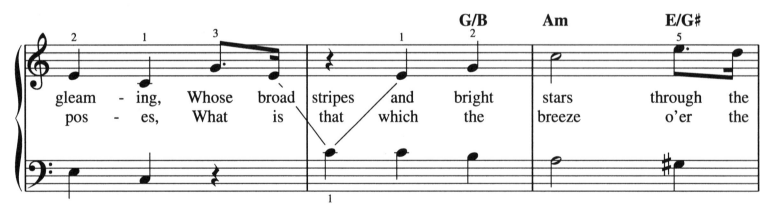

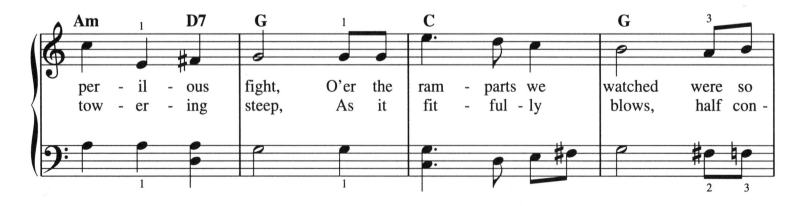

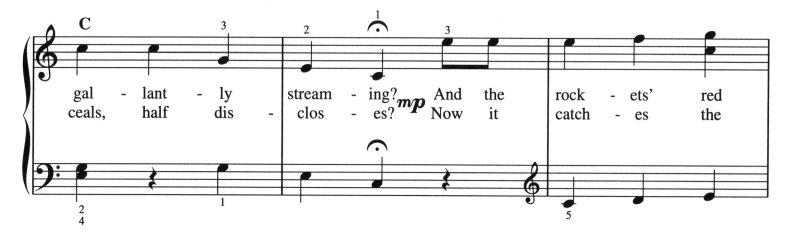

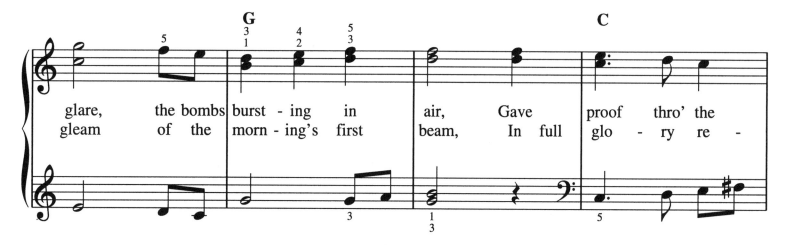

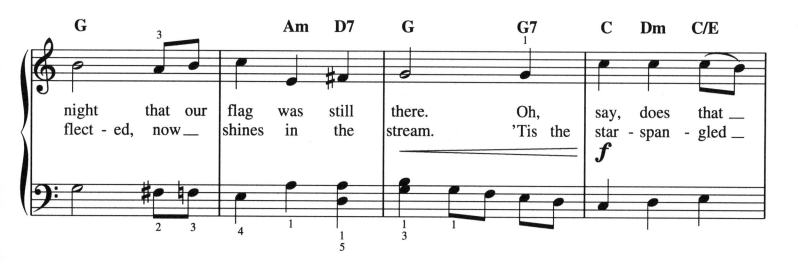

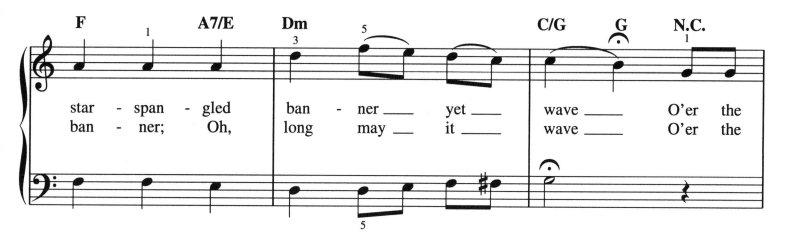

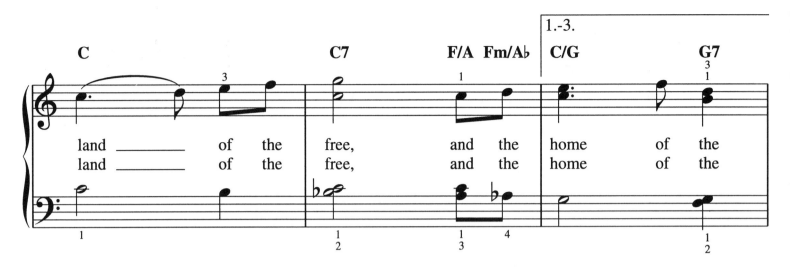

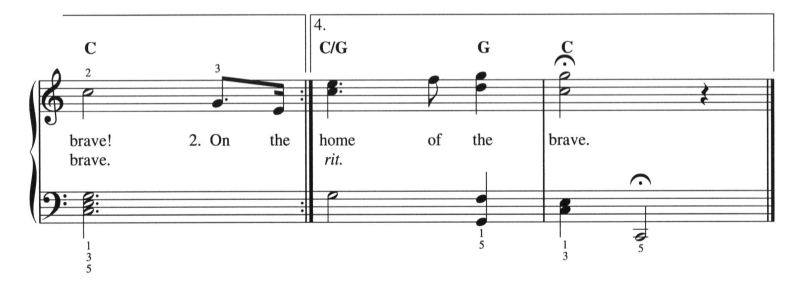

Additional Lyrics

3. And where is the band who so vauntingly swore,
   That the havoc of war and the battle's confusion
   A home and a country they'd leave us no more?
   Their blood has wash'd out their foul footstep's pollution.
   No refuge could save the hireling and slave
   From the terror of flight, or the gloom of the grave:
   And the star-spangled banner in triumph doth wave
   O'er the land of the free, and the home of the brave!

4. Oh, thus be it ever, when freemen shall stand
   Between their loved homes and the war's desolation;
   Blest with victory and peace, may the heaven-rescued land
   Praise the power that hath made and preserved us a nation!
   Then conquer we must, when our cause it is just,
   And this be our motto: "In God is our trust!"
   And the star-spangled banner in triumph shall wave,
   O'er the land of the free, and the home of the brave!

STARS AND STRIPES FOREVER

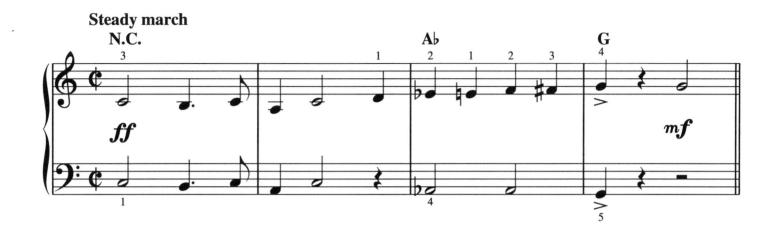

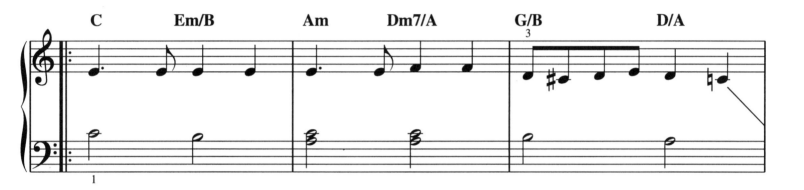

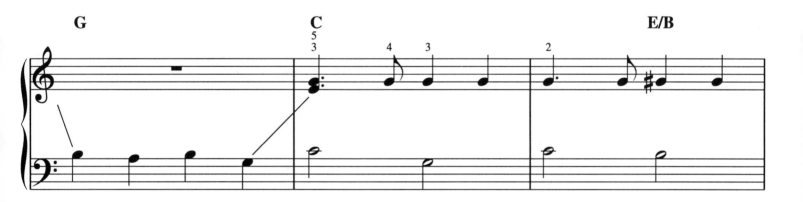

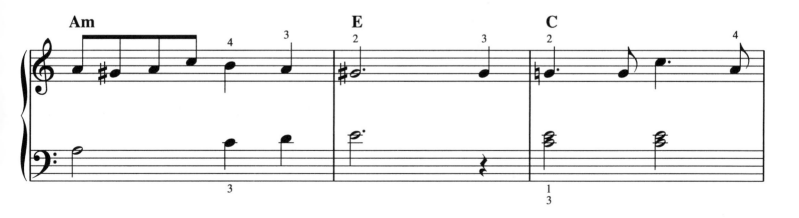

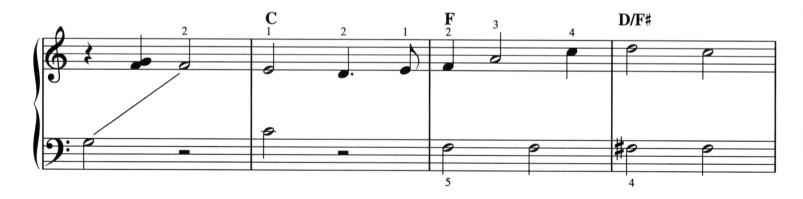

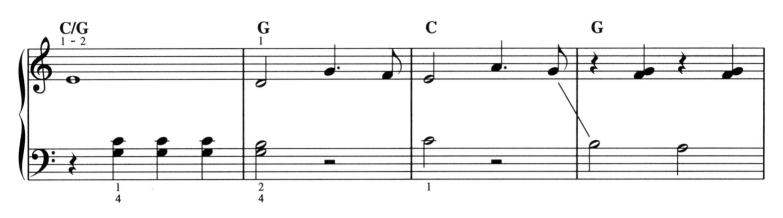

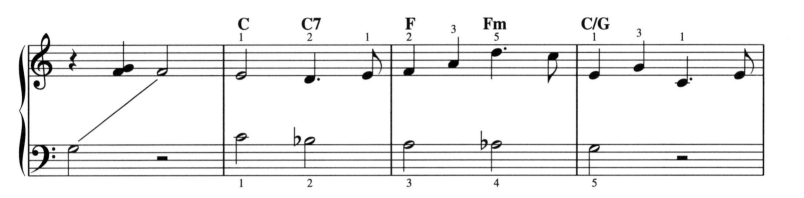

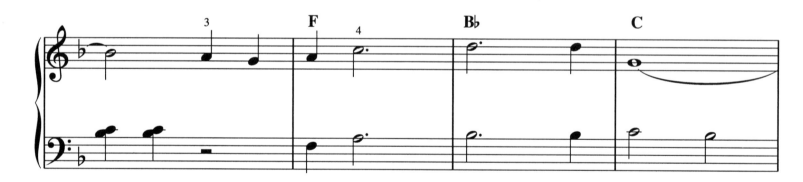

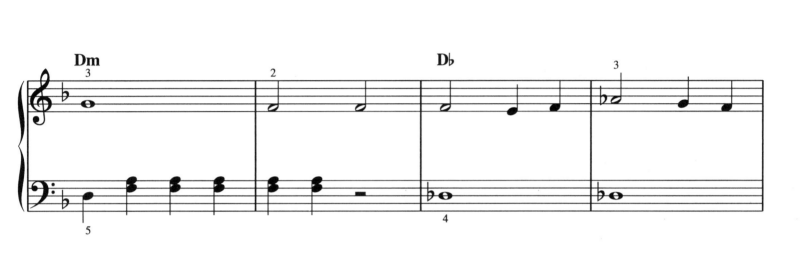

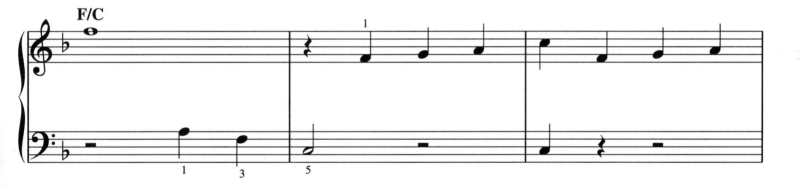

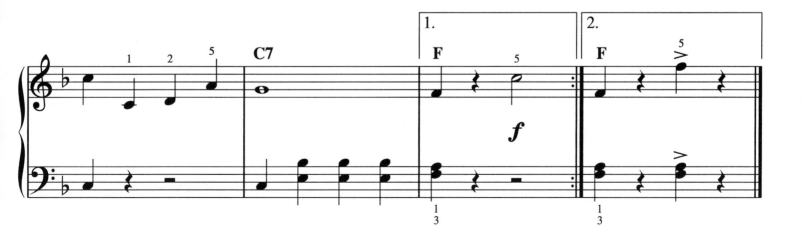

TRAMP, TRAMP, TRAMP

In the pris-on cell I sit think-ing
bat-tle front we stand when their

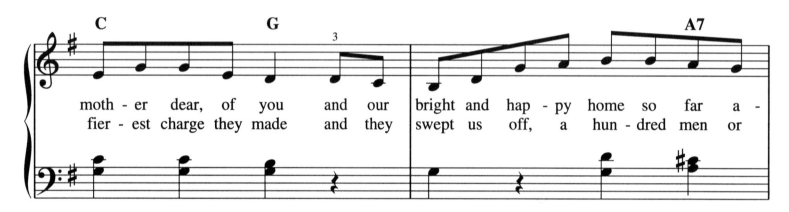

moth-er dear, of you and our bright and hap-py home so far a-
fier-est charge they made and they swept us off, a hun-dred men or

way. And the tears, they fill my eyes spite of
more. But be-fore we reached the lines they were

all that I can do, though I try to cheer my com-rades and be
beat-en back, dis-mayed. And we heard the cry of vic-t'ry o'er and

47

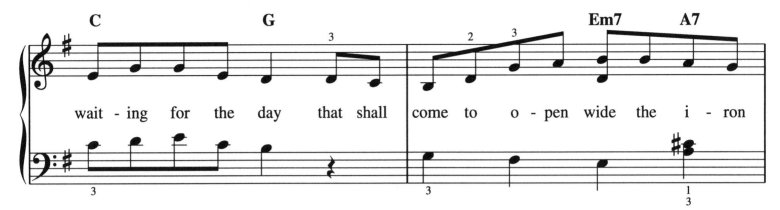

waiting for the day that shall come to o - pen wide the i - ron

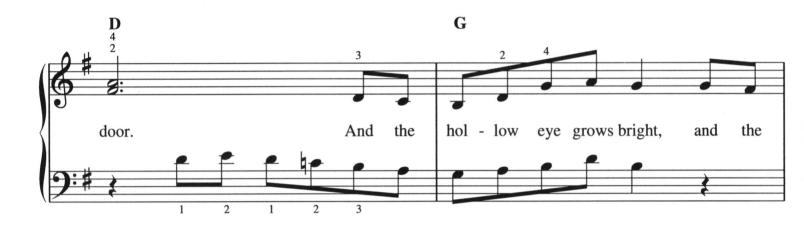

door. And the hol - low eye grows bright, and the

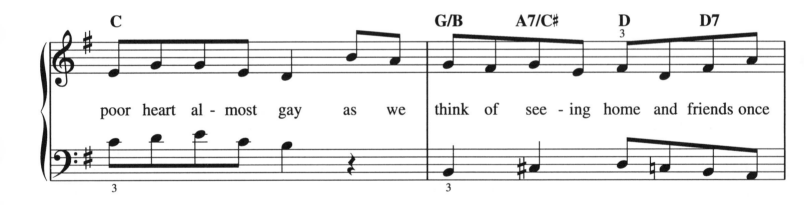

poor heart al - most gay as we think of see - ing home and friends once

more.

home.

THE YANKEE DOODLE BOY

Spirited march

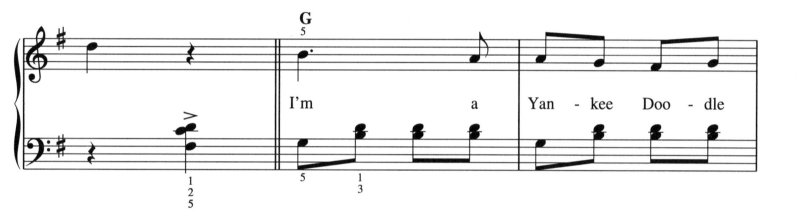

I'm   a   Yan - kee   Doo - dle

Dan   -   dy.   A   Yan   -   kee

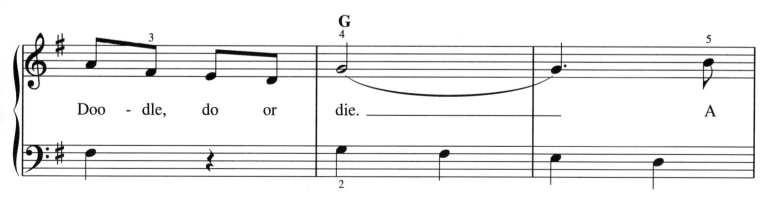

Doo - dle, do or   die. _____   A

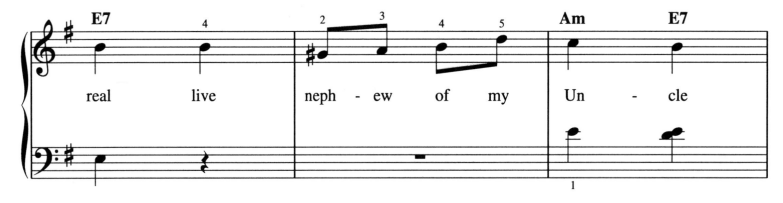

real live neph - ew of my Un - cle

Sam's, born on the Fourth of Ju -

ly. I've got a

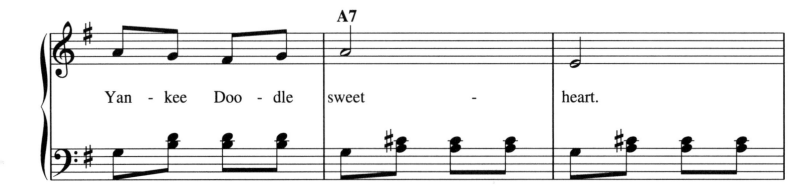

Yan - kee Doo - dle sweet - heart.

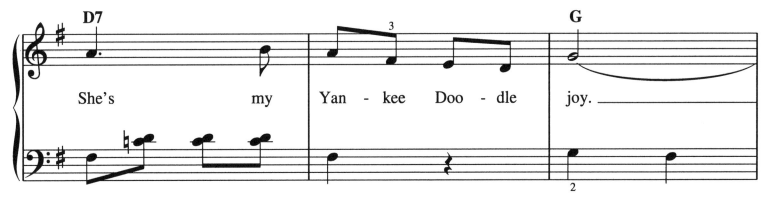

She's my Yan - kee Doo - dle joy. _____

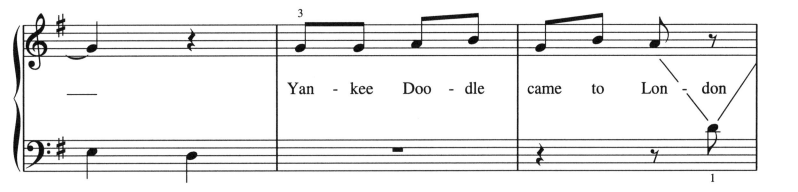

_____ Yan - kee Doo - dle came to Lon - don

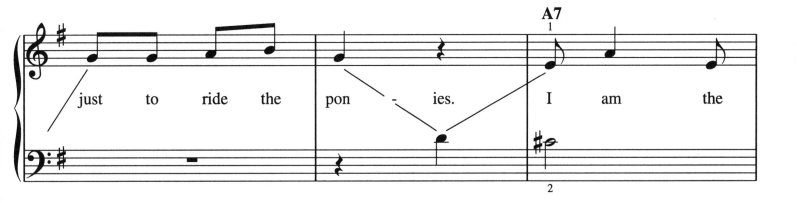

just to ride the pon - ies. I am the

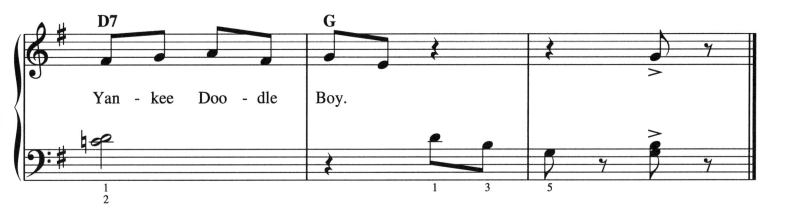

Yan - kee Doo - dle Boy.

WASHINGTON POST

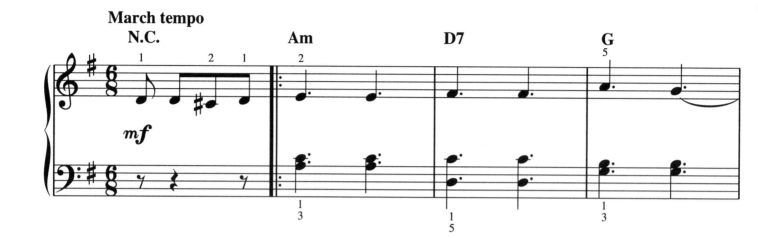

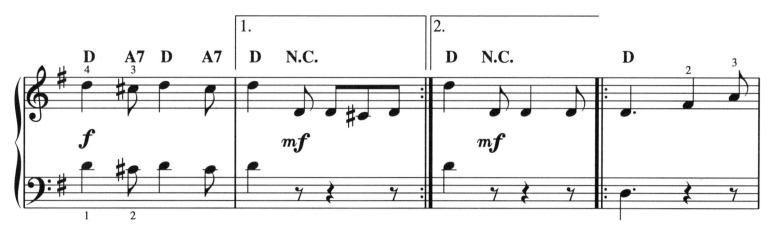

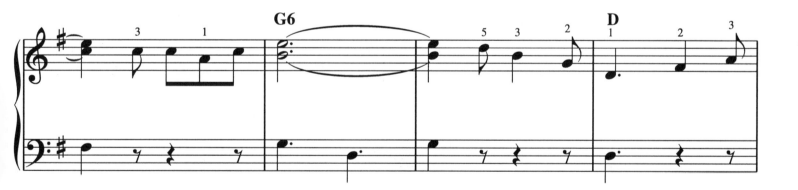

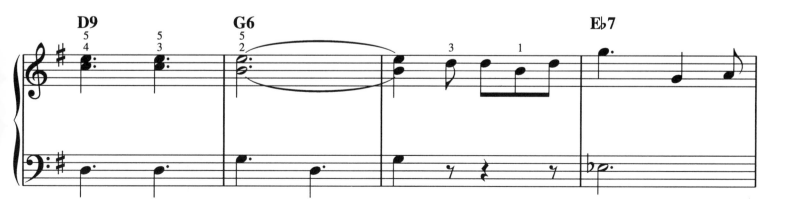

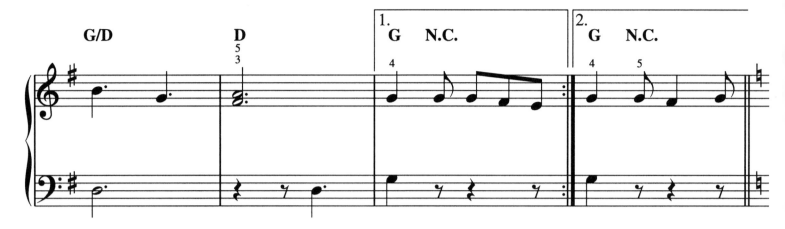

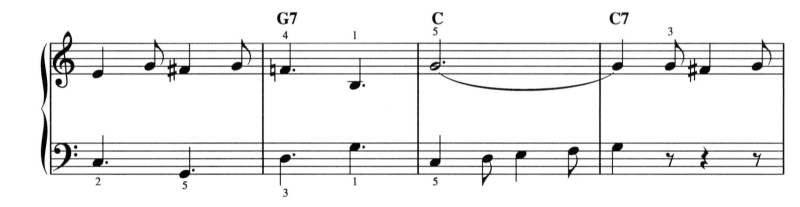

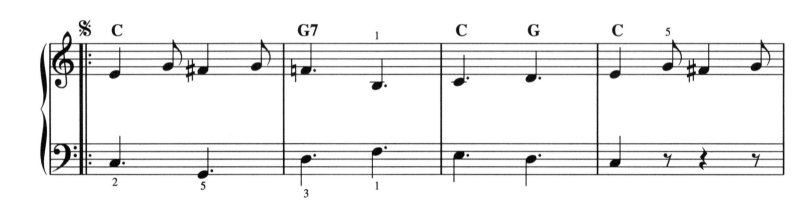

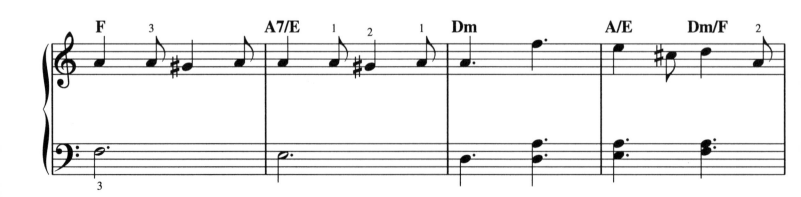

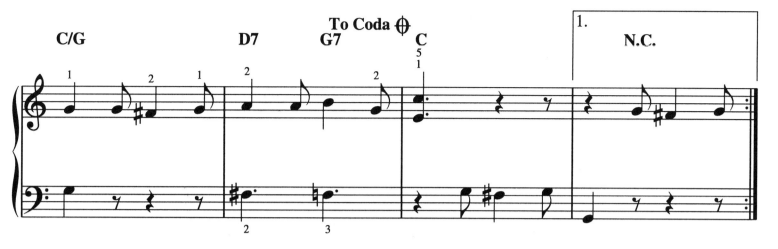

WHEN JOHNNY COMES MARCHING HOME

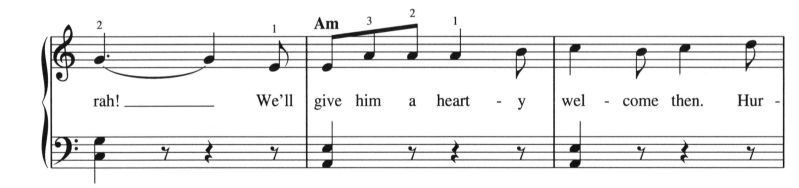

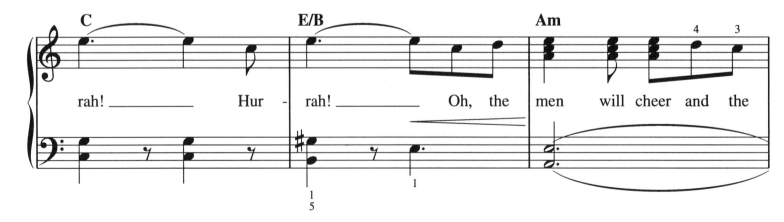

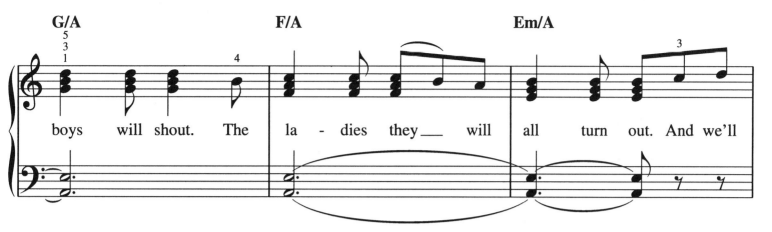

boys will shout. The la - dies they ___ will all turn out. And we'll

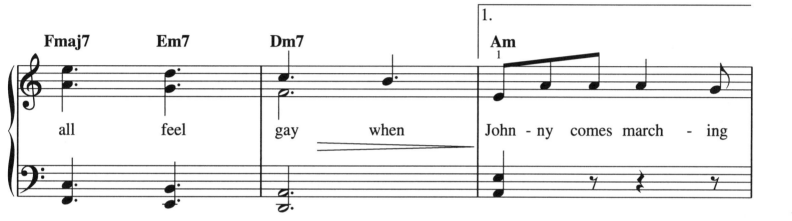

all feel gay when John - ny comes march - ing

home. When

John - ny comes march - ing home.

YOU'RE A GRAND OLD FLAG

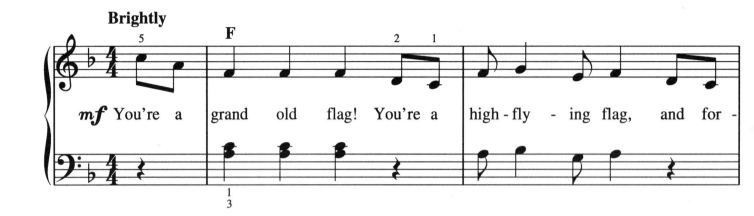

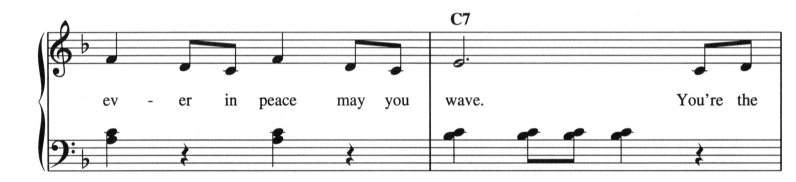

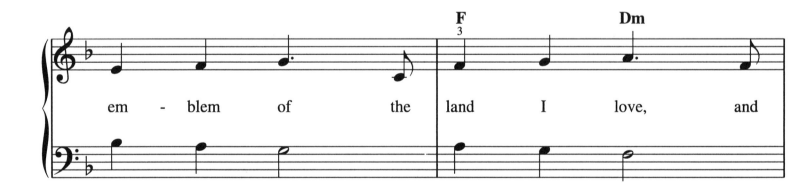

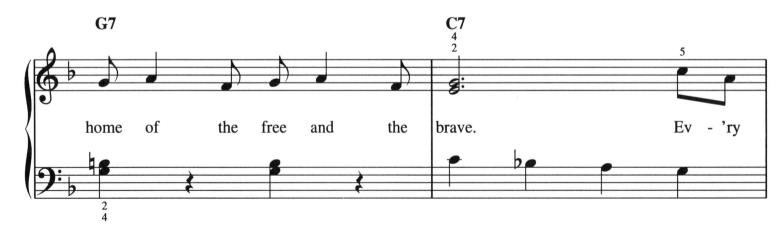

heart beats true un - der red, white and blue, where there's

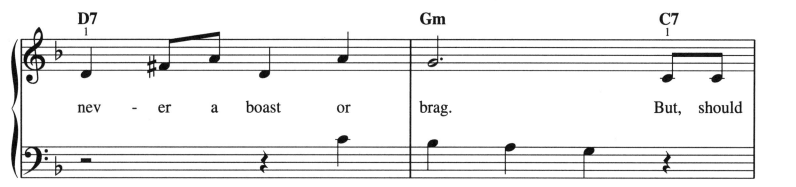

nev - er a boast or brag. But, should

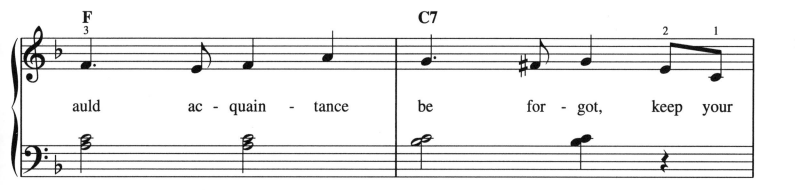

auld ac - quain - tance be for - got, keep your

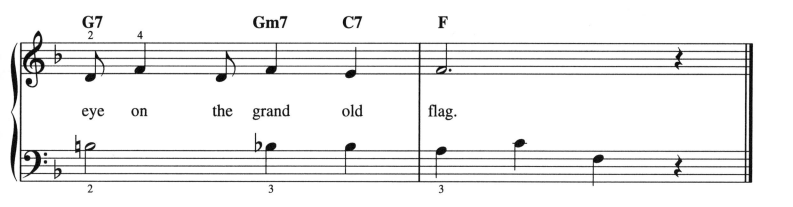

eye on the grand old flag.

THE YELLOW ROSE OF TEXAS

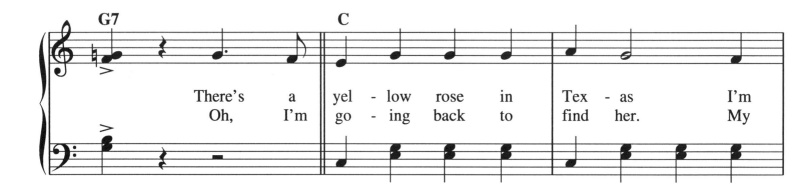

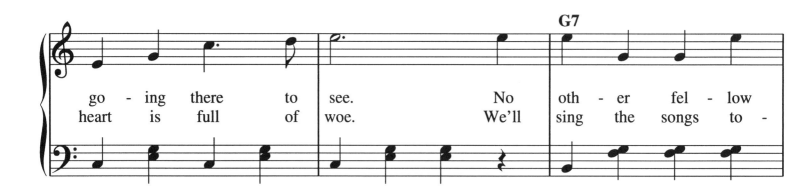

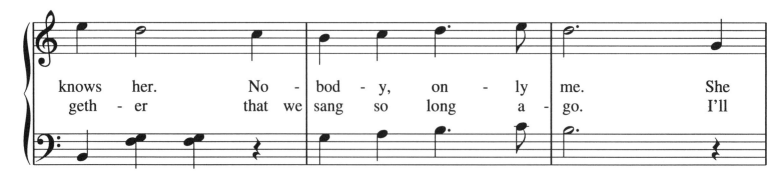

cried so when I left her. It like to broke my
pick the ban - jo gai - ly, and sing the songs of

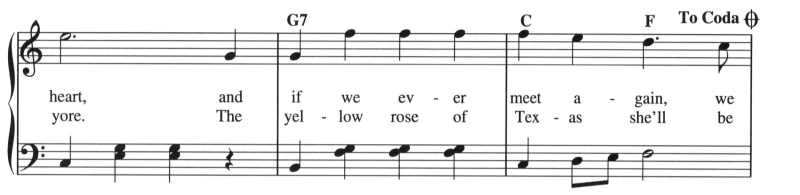

heart, and if we ev - er meet a - gain, we
yore. The yel - low rose of Tex - as she'll be

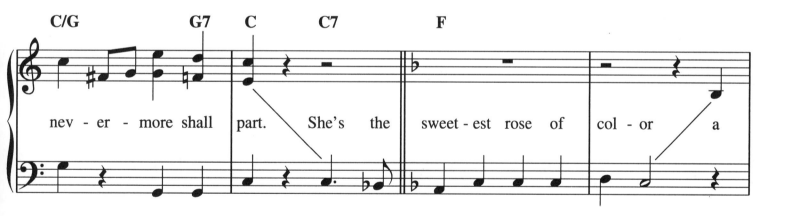

nev - er - more shall part. She's the sweet - est rose of col - or a

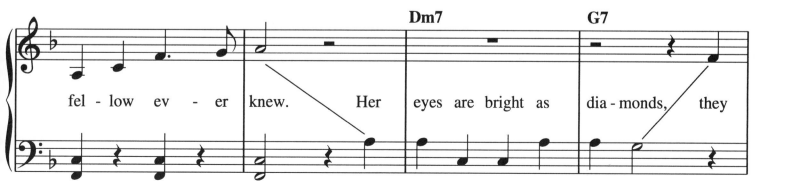

fel - low ev - er knew. Her eyes are bright as dia - monds, they

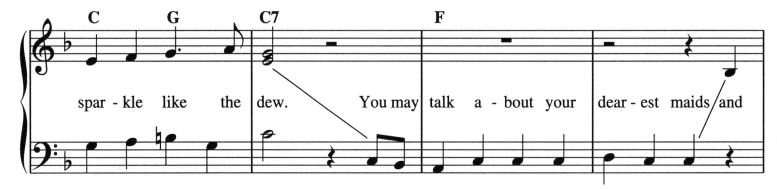

spar - kle like the dew. You may talk a - bout your dear - est maids and

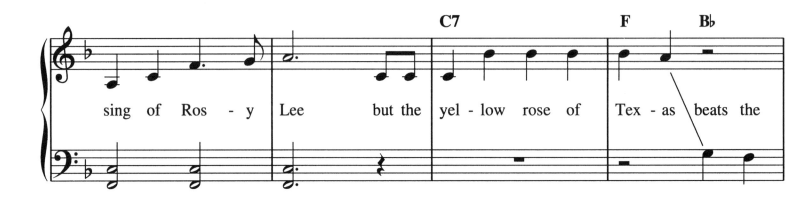

sing of Ros - y Lee but the yel - low rose of Tex - as beats the

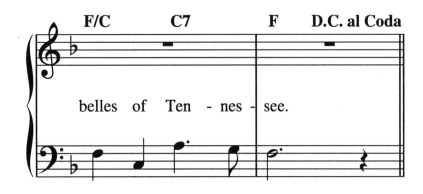

belles of Ten - nes - see.

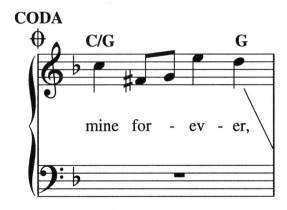

mine for - ev - er,

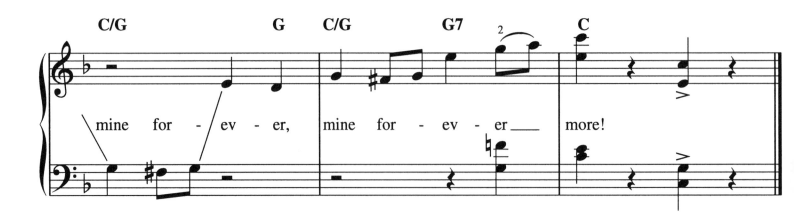

mine for - ev - er, mine for - ev - er more!

It's Easy To Play Your Favorite Songs with Hal Leonard Easy Piano Books

26 Easy Piano Hits Of The '90's
26 contemporary favorites, including: Baby Baby • Beauty And The Beast • Don't Know Much • Don't Let The Sun Go Down On Me • Emotions • How Am I Supposed To Live Without You • I Don't Have The Heart • To Be With You • Wind Of Change • and more.
00222550..$12.95

32 Easy Piano Great Hits Of Today
32 contemporary favorites, including: All This time • Baby Baby • Because I Love You (The Postman Song) • Don't Know Much • Every Heartbeat • How Can We Be Lovers • I Don't Have The Heart • Love Takes Time • Praying For Time • Release Me • Rhythm Of My Heart • Somewhere Out There • Vision Of Love • You're In Love • and more.
00222539 ....$12.95

Beauty And The Beast
A beautiful collector's edition of the music from Disney's latest classic, *Beauty And The Beast*. Complete with 8 songs and full color art from the movie. Songs include: Belle • Beauty And The Beast • Something There • and more.
00110003 ....$15.95

Movie Favorites For Easy Piano
Over 15 familiar theme songs, such as: Beauty And The Beast • Candle On The Water • Endless Love • Kokomo • The Rainbow Connection • Somewhere Out There • Unchained Melody • Under The Sea • and more.
00222551 ....$8.95

Miss Saigon
11 songs from this Broadway epic, including: The American Dream • The Heat Is On In Saigon • I'd Give My Life For You • The Last Night Of The World • Sun And Moon • and more.
00222537 ....$14.95

Rock N Roll For Easy Piano
arranged by Carol Klose
40 rock favorites for the piano, including: All Shook Up • At The Hop • Chantilly Lace • Great Balls Of Fire • Lady Madonna • The Shoop Shoop Song (It's In His Kiss) • The Twist • Wooly Bully • and more.
00222544..$12.95

The Gershwin Collection
arranged by Bill Boyd
A comprehensive collection of 39 of George and Ira's best, including: Fascinating Rhythm • How Long Has This Been Going On • I Got Rhythm • Let's Call The Whole Thing Off • Love Walked In • Nice Work If You Can Get It • 'S Wonderful • Someone To Watch Over Me • Strike Up The Band • They Can't Take That Away From Me • and more.
00222543..$12.95

Today's Love Songs
31 contemporary favorites, including: All I Ask Of You • Because I Love You • Don't Know Much • Endless Love • Forever And Ever, Amen • Here And Now • I'll Be Loving You Forever • Lost In Your Eyes • Love Without End, Amen • Rhythm Of My Heart • Unchained Melody • Vision Of Love • and more.
00222541..$14.95

The Best Of Paul McCartney
17 of his best, including: Band On The Run • Ebony and Ivory • Listen To What The Man Said • No More Lonely Nights • Say Say Say • Silly Love Songs • Uncle Albert/Admiral Halsey • With A Little Luck • and more.
00222548..$12.95

Best Of Cole Porter
Over 30 songs, including: Be A Clown • Begin The Beguine • Easy To Love • From This Moment On • In The Still Of The Night • Night And Day • So In Love • Too Darn Hot • You Do Something To Me • You'd Be So Nice To Come Home To • and more
00311576..$14.95

For more information, see your local music dealer, or write to:

HL® Hal Leonard Publishing Corporation

P.O. Box 13819 Milwaukee, Wisconsin 53213

Prices, book contents, and availability subject to change without notice